CAMOUFLAGED ANIMALS

Consultant: Steve Pollock
Graphic design: Sandra Brys

© Casterman 1993
First published in the UK in 1994 by
Belitha PressLtd
31 Newington Green, London N16 9PU
© First published in French by
Casterman 1993

ISBN 1 855 61 310 7

CAMOUFLAGED ANIMALS

Martine Duprez
Illustrated by Hélène Appell-Mertiny
Consultant: Steve Pollock

CONTENTS

Belitha Press

The success of any particular species of animal depends on its ability to survive. Animals do this by successfully finding food, reproducing and staying out of danger. When faced with a threat, an animal can fight, run away or stay completely still and hope not to be noticed. The animals that are most successful at staying still and hiding themselves are able to blend with their surroundings. This is the art of camouflage. In this book you will find nine examples of animals that can merge into the background in different ways and for different reasons.

Becoming invisible

The art of becoming invisible by merging into the surrounding environment is called camouflage. There are several ways that an animal can do this.

First, the animal may be the same colour as its background. During the course of their **evolution**, certain species have patterns on their bodies which make them difficult to see in their natural surroundings. Look, for example, at the green skin colour of those species which live in vegetation, the brown coat of those which live on dark ground, and the light coat of those which live in sand or snow. Marble, spotted or striped coats fit into a background of shade and light. For example, the spotted fur of the leopard makes it invisible in the wooded areas of the African plains.

INTRODUCTION

DIFFERENT
TYPES OF
CAMOUFLAGE

This change of skin or fur colour can also be temporary. Some animals can turn the colour of their surroundings as they change, and then change back again.

The brown fur of the stoat during the summer becomes white when the winter and snow arrive. This is a gradual change. Some animals can change their colour much faster. For example, the green tree frog, which in spite of its name, can vary its skin from brown to yellow instantly. The plaice can imitate the colour of the sand, stones or rocks over which it swims in a matter of minutes.

The best known example is the chameleon. Its skin changes to suit its surroundings as it creeps along branches towards its prey. However, the disguise is not always reliable. The chameleon's skin changes tones, because of special cells under the skin. They open or close according to temperature or brightness, but they also react to the mood of the chameleon. Anger or fright can often destroy the effects of the camouflage and turn the animal almost black!

Another way that animals camouflage themselves is by their shape. They have evolved to look like the surrounding environment. The stick insect is one of the best-known examples. These insects look like the twigs and stems of different vegetation. Leaf insects are part of the same family of animals. Naturally enough their bodies are shaped like leaves.

Loud camouflage?

There is a kind of camouflage that aims at confusing other animals. Certain defenceless insect species mimic the appearance of other more conspicuous insects. For example, the hover fly imitates the yellow and brown stripes of the wasp. Birds will leave the hover fly alone, thinking that it is a wasp and not wanting to be stung. This kind of camouflage is designed to avoid confrontation. It discourages would-be attackers.

Visual mimicry, based on forms and colours, is not the only way animals can deceive their enemies. Other forms of tricks are being discovered little by little by scientists. They are based on sounds, ultrasounds and smells. Did you know that certain orchids attract male insects by smelling exactly like the female insect? They smell particularly like the insects that help to pollinate the orchid. The art of deception is found in all sorts of unexpected places in nature.

THE STOAT

The stoat, a cousin of the ferret, is a cautious animal. It does not stay in one place for any length of time. Occasionally it will pause and take a look at its environment standing upright on its back paws. But then, fast as lightning, it will be off, crossing a road and leaping towards high grass. It slips through rocks and vegetation as swiftly and nimbly as a snake to find shelter in the heart of a thick bramble bush or in the crack of a dead tree. The only sign the stoat leaves behind on walls and rocks or where it crosses the road are its twisted and tapered droppings.

The stoat lives in a changing environment. The summers are warm and the winters are cold and it is often snowing. To fit in with its surroundings, its coat changes colour twice a year, in the springtime and in the autumn. Its fur turns white, when it snows, and brown in the summer months. Only the end of the stoat's tail remains black throughout the year. Some people believe that this protects it in winter from owls' attacks. The birds focus on the black spot which is clearly visible in the snow. They dive at the black spot, but find nothing to grab hold of. The stoat is able to dart off, just managing to escape.

The stoat's camouflage is not just for its own safety. It also benefits by becoming invisible to its **prey**. The stoat catches voles and mice, its favourite food, because it is neither seen nor heard.

LOCATION	GENERAL FEATURES	ENVIRONMENT	BEHAVIOUR

● The stoat is found in most of Europe (except in most of Spain, Portugal and Italy), northern USA, Greenland and northern Asia.

● In summer, the stoat's fur is brown on its back and white on its stomach. In winter, its coat becomes uniformly white. This happens in regions where the climate is very cold. It has a little peculiarity: its tail is permanently tipped with black, whatever the season.

● The total length of the male is between 28-43 cm (6-12 cm of which is the tail) and the female is 26-35 cm long (6-8 cm of which is the tail)

● The male weighs between 130-450 g: the female weighs between 130-280 g.

● It belongs to the *Mustelidae* family, like the weasel, badger, otter and pine marten.

● The stoat lives in fields, hedges, river banks, woods and thick bushes. It chooses hollows under trees' roots, low walls and cracks in rocks for shelter. It builds a nest inside its shelter, with grass, moss and leaves and sometimes even the skin and feathers of its prey.

● The stoat is usually **nocturnal** in winter and comes out in the daytime in summer.

CAMOUFLAGE

● In spring and autumn the stoat changes its coat to the colour of the countryside. In snowy winters its coat turns white, with the exception of the tip of its tail, which always stays black.

REPRODUCTION

● The stoat has one **litter** of between 4 to 9 offspring a year. The babies are born between April and May after a **gestation** period of 20-28 days.

DIET

● The stoat feeds mainly on voles, rats, mice and sometimes moles, shrews, birds' eggs, birds and fish.
● It does not hesitate to attack larger prey as well, like rabbits.

DANGERS AND MEASURES FOR CONSERVATION

● The stoat is often thought of as a pest. It is accused of stealing from farmyards and competing with farmers for game. As a result, people catch stoats in traps or shoot them.
● Another threat to the stoat is the destruction of its environment. Hedges, dead trees, hollow trunks and thick bushes are often destroyed and are therefore more difficult to find.
● People could help stoats by creating shelters and by controlling the numbers that are killed as pests.

THE LEOPARD

As dawn creeps on to the African **savannah**, the roars of lions and cackles of hyenas greet the new day. Antelopes start the day with a delicious meal of leaves that they tear from the branches of trees.

The tawny dappled coat of a leopard can hardly be seen in the tall grass. But the leopard is there, stalking its victim. It has picked on an antelope which has moved away from the others in the herd. Silently, the leopard glides along, moving from one bush to another, standing still each time the antelope looks around.

Suddenly the antelope straightens its head. Worried, it peers into the tall grass and sniffs the air: it smells danger. But it can't see anything in the yellow grass. The savannah appears still and quiet. Little by little, it becomes calm again and goes back to its meal. The leopard moves through the bushes and draws closer to the antelope. Crouching down, the leopard waits for the right moment. And then it leaps up. As the antelope looks for an escape, the leopard seizes it by the throat and suffocates it.

The leopard then carries the body of the antelope up into a tree where it starts its meal. Afterwards, the leopard rests sleepily in the shade of the acacia tree.

A jeep can be heard approaching along a nearby track. It stops close to the cat. The guide points out the leopard to the tourists in the jeep. With great difficulty, they finally distinguish the leopard lying in the dappled shade of the tree. Only the guide knew that the leopard was there. The tourists would have driven straight past it, because the leopard's camouflage is so good.

LOCATION	GENERAL FEATURES	ENVIRONMENT	BEHAVIOUR

● The African panther, more commonly known as the leopard, lives throughout the African continent, south of the Sahara.

● The leopard has a very light tawny coat, which is dappled with dark brown spots. Its tail is long and hairy. Its small, round ears are bordered by dark fur. Its claws are **retractable**.

● The leopard is about 70-95 cm high, from the ground to the top of its neck. The males weigh about 50 kg. The females are lighter and weigh about 40 kg.

● The leopard is a **carnivore**. It eats meat like other cats, such as tigers, lions and the domestic cat.

● The leopard lives in thorny thickets, along wooded rivers and in groves. It keeps clear of the plains. It can climb into trees to watch its prey or to rest. It is the only cat to carry its prey up into the trees and may even eat it there.

● Leopards normally live on their own. They tend to live in a particular area and mark out their territory with scent. Being nocturnal animals, they rest during the day and hunt at night.

14

CAMOUFLAGE

● The leopard's coat is a permanent, natural camouflage, because its spots merge perfectly with vegetation, rocky countryside or shaded areas.

REPRODUCTION

● The female gives birth to anything between 1 to 6 cubs after a gestation period of 95-105 days.

DIET

● Antelopes are the leopard's favourite prey. It will also eat monkeys, birds, wild pigs and rodents.

DANGERS AND MEASURES FOR CONSERVATION

● The leopard has always been hunted as a trophy and for its fur.
● Today the leopard is protected by an international agreement, the Washington Convention, which bans the trade of leopard skins.
● However, the leopard is still hunted by poachers and is also endangered because its natural habitats are being destroyed.

THE HEDGEHOG

The oak tree's shadow is picked out by the brightness of the moon's light. A bat swoops around chasing insects. The peaceful night is disturbed only by frogs, croaking in the distance.

Another sound disturbs the peace. Humming and scratching noises seem to be coming from a bush. The grass moves and a hedgehog appears. Stocky and covered with needles, it moves with small, quick steps. Every once in a while, it stops and sniffs the smells on the damp ground, then carries on searching for its prey. But a sudden noise frightens it. It completely stops, ready to roll into a ball and defends itself from attack by exposing only its needles.

Nothing can hurt the hedgehog without pricking itself first.

All is quiet again. So the hedgehog carries on its search for food. It snuffles along the hedge, exploring the nooks in search of insects, plump **larvae** or slugs. It would be specially lucky to find eggs or a sleeping frog.

Hedgehogs are often seen on the roads, because insects rest for the night on the warm tar. So roads are a good source of food. However, because the hedgehog's defence is to curl into a ball and not move when frightened, they are often killed by cars. Drivers find it difficult to spot hedgehogs because of their dark colouring. So the hedgehog's camouflage and defences are no protection for it on the roads. In any other dangerous situation the hedgehog is served well by its camouflage and needles.

LOCATION	GENERAL FEATURES	ENVIRONMENT	BEHAVIOUR

● The hedgehog can be found throughout Europe.

● The hedgehog has a squat body, a pointed snout and small round ears. Its tail is hardly visible. It is covered with up to 6,000 dark brown needles, which have spots of white on the bottom and the top. Its stomach is covered by a rather soft light brown coat. It measures 20-30 cm in length, of which 2-3.5 cm is its tail. Its weight varies from between 400 g-1.4 kg. It is a member of the **insectivore** group, which includes shrews and moles, which all eat small animals, including insects, worms and other invertebrates.

● Hedgehogs prefer to live in forests, fields, hedges, parks and gardens.
● Each animal has its own territory, varying in size from 4-40 hectares.

● The hedgehog is especially active at dusk and during the night. In the day it shelters in a large nest of leaves, grass and moss.
● It **hibernates** from October to April.

CAMOUFLAGE

● The hedgehog is grey-brown, which helps to hide it during the night. But when it does move it makes a lot of noise.

● However, in moments of danger, it can curl up into a tight ball and is able to protect itself with its armour of needles.

REPRODUCTION

● The female has one or two litters a year. It has between 2 to 10 babies, after a gestation period of around 35 days.

DIET

● It feeds on insects, earthworms, snails and slugs. But it also eats small rodents, berries and fruit.

DANGERS AND MEASURES FOR CONSERVATION

● In the past the hedgehog was hated by country people. They thought that it used to cling to the udders of cows and suck out milk. This is wrong.

● Today, the biggest danger to hedgehogs are cars. Thousands of hedgehogs are killed on the roads every year.

● The hedgehog also suffers from the spreading of insecticides. Not only does this kill its food, but when the hedgehog eats a poisoned insect it too can die.

We can protect the hedgehog in several ways:

● by reducing and restricting the use of **insecticides** and weed killers.

● by protecting its habitat by looking after hedges, forests and parks.

THE CHAMELEON

The whirring of **cicadas** resounds around the hot pine wood. The animals and flowers of the wood seem to wilt under the fierce heat of the sun. Scarcely visible against the dry bush, a camouflaged chameleon advances very slowly towards an unsuspecting insect.

The insect, unaware of the danger that is looming, continues to gather nectar. Suddenly, the chameleon shoots out its tongue. But it misses! The insect is even faster and moves a little further away.

Even though this attack hasn't succeeded, the chameleon is not put off and very slowly starts to hunt all over again.

The next time, it catches its prey. The insect victim, held in the sticky liquid that coats the end of the chameleon's tongue, disappears into the chameleon's mouth.

The chameleon's camouflage allows it to merge with its surroundings, which means it can move around unnoticed. But this disguise is not always reliable. When angry or afraid, the chameleon's skin can turn black so it is no longer hidden.

LOCATION	GENERAL FEATURES	ENVIRONMENT	BEHAVIOUR

● The European chameleon originates from North Africa. It can be found in southern Spain and Crete.

● Normally soft green, the skin of the chameleon can change colour rapidly and become dark brown.
● The length of its body can reach about 30 cm.
● It has two protruding eyes that can move independently from each other. They are protected by scales. It also has a long tail that easily grips branches.
● Its feet have two toes on one side and three on the other. This gives the chameleon a good grip on branches and makes it very agile.
● The chameleon is a **reptile**.

● The chameleon lives in dry places and brushwood. It generally rests perched on a well-lit branch.

● The chameleon is active during the day. It hunts alone and moves very slowly.
● During the mating season, chameleons leave their normal territory and go in search of other chameleons.

CAMOUFLAGE

● The changes in the chameleon's skin colour are caused by pigment cells. These cells expand or contract in reaction to the light and temperature around the animal, or to the mood of the chameleon.

REPRODUCTION

● The female lays between 9-30 eggs. These are buried in the ground and hatch after 250 days of **incubation**. This egg laying is exhausting and many females die after they have done it.

DIET

● A chameleon mainly feeds on insects. Settled on a branch it waits for its prey to land. As soon as it detects an insect, it slowly approaches it and shoots out its tongue. The insect gets caught in the sticky substance on the end of the tongue and is drawn into the chameleon's mouth.

DANGERS AND MEASURES FOR CONSERVATION

● The number of chameleons is decreasing all the time. The species is heading towards extinction. These animals are dying out because their habitat is being destroyed. Pine forests are being cleared for summer tourists. Elsewhere the spread of insecticides has killed off mosquitoes, the chameleon's main food.
● Chameleons are on the list of species protected by the Washington Convention. This agreement checks the trade of threatened species.

Although the spring sun has shone, the day only just gets warm before dusk begins. In the fading light, green tree frogs start to croak in chorus. The males are courting the females. These croaks can be heard for hundreds of metres around and they betray the frogs' presence. Their skin, which is the same colour as the leaves they live among, makes them practically invisible.

THE GREEN TREE FROG

A group of young people, wearing wellington boots and carrying buckets and torches, walks along the road nearby. When they reach the part of the road that is near the pond inhabited by the green tree frogs, they turn towards the verge. They lean over and squat among the grass, very close to a strange home-made construction of a long leaf stretched between two pieces of wood.

Behind the leaf, dozens of green tree frogs are trapped. They are trying to cross the road to get to the pond. But this artificial barrier stops them from jumping on to the road and ending up crushed under the tyres of a car.

The young **conservationists** delicately put the **amphibians** into their buckets. Transported like this, the tree frogs cross the road safely. As soon as they are dropped on the ground the other side of the road, they head straight for the pond, their mating ground.

LOCATION	GENERAL FEATURES	ENVIRONMENT	BEHAVIOUR

● The green tree frog is found all over Europe, except in the Nordic Countries and the British Isles. It does not live in the Balearic Islands.

● Despite its name, the green tree frog's colour can vary, from green to yellow to brown and sometimes even blue, depending on the frog's surroundings.
● The males have a brown-grey vocal sac in the breeding season.
● The male's back foot is webbed with two to three toes. It has suction pads on every toe to help it cling to slippery vegetation.
● Its body measures 3.5-5 cm long.
● Green tree frogs are amphibians.

● It lives mainly in grassy areas and is fond of woods, bushes and grass. During the day it settles in leaves or on bulrushes.
● During the breeding period, it lives in the still waters of ponds.

● The green tree frog is especially active at night. It lives in large groups called colonies. Its croaking can be heard for hundreds of metres around.
● It hibernates at the beginning of October in the banks of ponds or under rocks.

CAMOUFLAGE	REPRODUCTION	DIET	DANGERS AND MEASURES FOR CONSERVATION

● To escape its enemies, the frog stays absolutely still and the colour of its skin blends into its immediate environment. When it sticks to a green leaf, it is virtually invisible.

● The green tree frog lays between 800-1,000 eggs in one night. Several groups of eggs are left on water plants. At the end of about two weeks, tadpoles emerge from the eggs. After three months, these tadpoles turn into frogs. This change of appearance from young to adult is called metamorphosis.

● It feeds on snails, spiders, little beetles and insects.

● The green tree frog is disappearing. Its natural environment is being destroyed and marshes are drying up. Pollution is also killing the frog, as rubbish and chemicals are poured into marshy areas. It is also being threatened by trade. People are catching the frogs to sell them to laboratories. During times of **migration** the frogs are also killed by cars as they cross the road.
● The Berne Convention protects all amphibians in European countries. It makes sure that each country obeys its rules.
● Because these frogs migrate, people have studied their routes and made sure that they are safely transported across roads, as in the story. This stops them from being run over by cars.

STICK INSECTS

The afternoon is drawing to a close. A light breeze shakes the big larch tree and cools the hot air.

The children insisted on a walk before dinner. They ran through the village and climbed the rocky path towards the little woods. Julian held the hand of his little sister Lucy firmly. When they ran out of breath, they decided to rest before going to the top of the hill.

Exhausted and hot, they collapsed next to the brushwood that borders the path, frightening the cicadas that had settled there for their nightly concert.

Lying on his back, Julian looked at the branches and twigs of the small shrubs swinging above him. One twig in particular intrigued him. Leaning on his elbows, he peered closely at the branch.

He suddenly realised that it seemed to be alive and was eating a leaf. Fascinated, he showed his little sister. She laughed and told him what it was.

"Stupid idiot. It's a stick insect." Julian defended himself by saying, "Well, it's not surprising that I've never seen one before. They are so well camouflaged!"

LOCATION	GENERAL FEATURES	ENVIRONMENT	BEHAVIOUR

● There are more than 2,000 kinds, or species, of stick insect throughout the tropical regions of Asia, Africa and America. They are also found around the Mediterranean coastline.

● Some stick insects can reach up to 40 cm in length.
● The stick insect is part of a group of animals called plasmids. Leaf insects belong to the same group. They disguise themselves by looking like leaves.
● All the plasmids have certain common characteristics. They all have a small head with thread-like antennae, three pairs of legs that are long, and small wings or no wings at all. Their colour varies from brown to green.

● Stick insects live in trees, bushes and brushwood.

● Stick insects are nocturnal animals that settle on low plants during the day. At nightfall they become active, but they never appear to move quickly.

CAMOUFLAGE

● The stick insect looks exactly like a little twig. It moves around totally unnoticed. Some species are more refined and are able to change their colour. Others hang in empty space and swing in the wind like real twigs.

REPRODUCTION

● There are more females than males in this species (1 male for every 1,000 females). This explains why there is often **asexual reproduction**. The females lay unfertilised eggs. These are hidden on the ground or in cracks in rocks. The incubation period is very long. The stick insect reaches the adult stage after a series of changes. It starts as an egg, from which hatches a young stick insect. This moults several times before becoming an adult.

DIET

● All stick insects eat plants, especially leaves. Their mouthparts grind their food.

DANGERS AND MEASURES FOR CONSERVATION

● European stick insects have hardly been studied up until now. Although they suffer in forest fires, it seems that they are not endangered. However, they continually have to move back into burnt lands and this is a very slow process.

Some ancient Latin authors gave this advice to bee keepers who had lost their swarm, 'Place the dead body of an animal in an unused cowshed. You will find that your bees will come and eat there.'

How many bee keepers followed this advice? No one can say. But only the very stupid would have believed this wrong information.

THE DRONE FLY

The insects that eat from the carcass of a dead animal don't produce any honey. But there is a reason for all this bad advice. The insects that lay their eggs on dead and rotting meat look like bees.

These 'bees' are in fact drone flies. They are easily mistaken for honey bees, because their colouring and size are almost identical. So much so that certain birds that try to avoid swallowing bees are afraid of this fake bee, just in case it stings. But the drone fly has no sting and is therefore totally harmless. Its camouflage saves it from the beaks of hungry birds.

LOCATION	GENERAL FEATURES	ENVIRONMENT	BEHAVIOUR
● The drone fly is found all over the world, especially in Europe and North America, where it has the nickname 'bee-fly'.	● The drone fly looks very like the bee. It has the same kind of colouring and is the same size. However, that is where the similarities end. ● The drone fly has two wings whereas the bee has four. The bee seems to be made up of two distinct parts with a wasp-like waist, whereas the drone fly has no distinctive waist. The big antennae of the bee twitch as they get near nectar. The drone fly's antennae are still. And of course, most importantly, the drone fly has no sting. ● It is part of the hover fly family.	● The drone fly lives in grassy areas, like gardens and fields.	● Active during the day, the drone fly plays an important part in the pollination of flowers.

The bee

The drone fly

CAMOUFLAGE	REPRODUCTION	DIET	DANGERS AND MEASURES FOR CONSERVATION
● Certain birds avoid the drone fly because it looks like a bee, and so they think it will sting.	● After mating the fly lays its eggs in a muddy pond or a pool of liquid manure. The larvae spend the winter there, before changing in spring to become flies. They can breathe air through a siphon so they can live in stagnant water.	● Like the bee, drone flies consume nectar and pollen. The larvae feed on decaying matter, such as rotting vegetation or dead animals.	● This species is abundant and common. As long as manure and rubbish are around, so too is the drone fly.

Take a look at the skin of the plaice and you will notice that it has a slightly dappled quality. The plaice may be able to survive in the sea by disguising itself, but that doesn't save it from the nets of fishermen.

Some scientists are interested in the plaice's skilful disguise. One particularly spectacular experiment has been done by scientists in a laboratory. Researchers put a chess board on the bottom of an aquarium with a plaice in it. They then leave it for a couple of hours.

THE PLAICE

When they come back what has happened? The plaice has reproduced a superb chess board on the top part of its body, which faces the surface.

In the plaice's natural environment of the sea, the changes on its skin are less sensational. It imitates patterns in the mud or gravel on which it has settled by automatically changing its skin tones. In this way it stays hidden from its predators. It also uses this camouflage to sneak up on its prey undetected.

LOCATION	GENERAL FEATURES	ENVIRONMENT	BEHAVIOUR

● The plaice is found as far north as the Barents Sea in the Arctic Ocean down to southern Spain and throughout the western Mediterranean.

● The plaice is a flat fish. Its eyes are on the upper side of its body. Its underside is off-white. The upper part of the body that faces the sea reflects the colours and textures of the fish's surroundings. It is often dotted with round red or orange spots.
● Plaice used to be found measuring over a metre long. Today they rarely reach 80 cm.

● The plaice lives on the bottom of the sea in sand, mud or gravel. They are found at a sea depth of up to 120 metres, but more often at depths of around 27-73 metres.

● The plaice hunts by hiding and waiting. Thanks to its camouflage it is well hidden from predators.

CAMOUFLAGE

● This fish is able to vary its skin colour due to special cells under the skin called chromatophores.

REPRODUCTION

● Each female lays up to 500,000 eggs that drift around with the sea currents. The eggs hatch into larvae in 17 days.

● Young larvae have eyes on either side of their body and in a short time one eye moves over to join the other. The young fish then flips on to its side ready to live on the sea bed.

DIET

● Plaice feed on a number of **invertebrates**, such as worms, snails and shellfish, such as shrimps.

DANGERS AND MEASURES FOR CONSERVATION

● The plaice is threatened by intensive fishing, which drastically reduces the number of individuals in a species.
● It is also a victim of pollution from chemicals poured into the sea by industrial factories. Fishermen are finding more and more diseased fish in their nets.
● What is the solution? There are now some laws that stop intensive fishing. To stop pollution in the sea, it is vitally important to limit the amount of industrial waste that finds its way into the sea.

THE ALPINE PTARMIGAN

The low and wispy sky is filled with snow, coating the land with a soft white layer that muffles the slightest noise. The snow-capped summits of the mountains are silent. In this winter scene of complete whiteness, a raucous and cawing cry suddenly breaks into the stillness.

Looking quickly at the spot where the noise came from, you may be able to distinguish a bird. It is slightly larger than a partridge and white, with only a few small black spots on its feathers. It is an alpine ptarmigan. The bird is well protected against its enemies because it is almost invisible in the snow. It is also completely adapted to life in the cold. It digs through the snow to find food in the vegetation underneath, and it builds a sort of little igloo that serves as a winter shelter.

In the spring when the snow has melted, the male displays its white winter feathers to attract females. Its plumage makes a very handsome contrast with the countryside. The males defend their territory fiercely against intruders, especially other males, who are rivals for the females.

With summer, the countryside changes. And the ptarmigan does as well. It becomes tawny grey with little dark brown spots. This makes it difficult to distinguish from the stone chippings on the ground or the moss, lichens and heathers of the **tundra**.

The alpine ptarmigan is well prepared when protecting itself from its natural enemies, but no change of feather colour will keep it safe from human hunters.

LOCATION	GENERAL FEATURES	ENVIRONMENT	BEHAVIOUR

The male's plumage in summer

The female's plumage in autumn

● The alpine ptarmigan lives in Iceland, northern Norway, northern Scotland (650 metres above sea level) and in the French Alps and Pyrenees (2,000 metres above sea level).

● The alpine ptarmigan is slightly larger than a partridge. It is about 35 cm long.
● Its wings stay white all year round and its tail stays black. But its body changes three times depending on the season: white in winter, tawny grey, spotted with dark brown in both spring and summer, and finely spotted grey in autumn.
● The ptarmigan is part of the *Tetraonidae* (grouse family).

● The alpine ptarmigan lives in mountainous and rocky regions as well as in the tundra.

● The alpine ptarmigan does not travel very much, and it marks out its territory. The male fiercely defends its territory during the mating season.

CAMOUFLAGE

● The feathers of this bird change colour according to the season. As soon as the first snow falls the grey autumn feathers turn white, with the exception of the tail feathers which stay black. In the summer the ptarmigan is tawny grey. It therefore merges perfectly with its background at all times.

REPRODUCTION

● Between May and July the females lay about 6-10 lightly spotted eggs.
● The incubation lasts for around 21-24 days.

DIET

● It feeds on young plant growth, buds, berries and wild grains, but also every now and then snails, worms and insects.

DANGERS AND MEASURES FOR CONSERVATION

● The population of alpine ptarmigans, which is small anyway, is on the decline.
● The ptarmigan is hunted in Great Britain.
● Tourist activities, such as skiing (in the Alps, the Pyrenees and the Cairngorms in Scotland), disturb the ptarmigan's mountain habitats.

GLOSSARY

A

amphibians: cold-blooded animals that live both in water and on land.

asexual reproduction: a form of reproduction that needs only a female parent.

C

carnivore: a meat-eating animal.

cicadas: insects that make a chirping noise at night.

conservationist: someone who protects animals and their environments.

E

evolution: the way living things change over long periods of time in response to changes in the environment.

G

gestation: the length of time it takes for offspring to develop inside the mother.

H

hibernate: to pass the winter in a state similar to sleep.

I

incubation: the length of time it takes for offspring to develop in the egg.

insecticides: chemical poisons which kill insects.

insectivores: animals that eat insects.

invertebrates: animals that have no backbone.

L

larvae: an immature form of an animal that will develop into the adult form.

litter: a group of young that are produced at one birth.

M

migration: a journey from habitat to another at set times of the year, often to find food.

N

nocturnal: being active at night.

P

prey: an animal that is hunted as food by another, called a predator.

R

reptile: a cold-blooded, scaly-skinned animal with a back-bone (a vertebrate) that lays eggs on land.

retractable: something which can be pulled in and out of the way.

S

savannah: open grasslands with scattered trees, usually found in Africa.

T

tundra: a huge, cold, treeless area between the Arctic ice cap and the wooded parts of northern Canada and Europe.

V

vertebrates: animals that have backbones.T

INDEX

Printed in Belgium.